contents

NZ, Canada, US and UK readers
Please note that Australian cup and spoon
measurements are metric. A quick conversion
guide appears on page 63.

2
kids' party
sanity savers

Little kids' parties might be fun for the little kids but they're hardly relaxing for the adults in charge. Here are some suggestions to help relieve the stress.

◆ Remove toothpicks, skewers and any other sharp objects from food before you serve it. Always make sure an adult is in the room while young children are eating, in case a child chokes.

◆ Send out invitations in plenty of time to allow guests' parents to change their plans if necessary, and stipulate starting and finishing times.

◆ Make sure there are enough adults in the house to supervise a party for young children.

◆ Plan to have some grown-up food (and tea, coffee or wine) in case some of the more anxious parents come early to pick up their children.

◆ Wrap up small presents or bags of sweets with a guest's name on each one and give them out when the children leave. If you have balloons, give each child one to take home with him. Be vigilant when balloons are about. Once popped they can be a danger to young children — if they put the bits of coloured plastic in their mouth, they could choke.

◆ Cut the party cake into thin slices to give to the guests at the party (most children will have had enough to eat by the time the cake comes around), and wrap up another slice for each of the children to take home.

◆ The food shouldn't be too hot. Just-cooked sausage rolls and cocktail frankfurts, for example, can burn little mouths.

◆ Anticipate problems, especially with party games. There might be squabbles about who got to a chair first in musical chairs, for example. Explain the rules before the games begin.

◆ Don't give yourself so much work to do in the kitchen that you can't sit back and enjoy the fun. Prepare as much food as you can in advance.

◆ Have plenty of large sturdy paper napkins at hand to wipe faces, hands and spills on clothes.

◆ Don't be over-adventurous when planning the food. Many young children are picky eaters and won't be interested in black olive dip.

◆ Try to serve at least a few types of healthy food. A bowl of vegetables cut into matchsticks with a simple dip might not be the first thing a child will head for, but if it looks colourful and appetising, you'll probably find it will disappear in time.

◆ A buffet is best for older children, but small children will be more comfortable (and make less

mess) sitting at low tables or on cushions on the floor.

◆ Young children need constant supervision, but leave older children in peace at least some of the time during the party, only checking from time to time that everything is alright.

vegie nachos

1 tablespoon olive oil

1 medium brown onion (150g), chopped finely

1 clove garlic, crushed

425g can chopped tomatoes

420g can Mexibeans

240g packet corn chips

1 cup (125g) coarsely grated cheddar cheese

1 large avocado (320g)

1/2 cup (125ml) sour cream

1 tablespoon lemon juice

Heat oil in medium saucepan; cook onion and garlic, stirring, until onion is soft. Add undrained tomatoes and beans; simmer, uncovered, about 15 minutes or until mixture thickens slightly. **Just** before serving, place corn chips on a large ovenproof plate; pour over bean mixture. Sprinkle with cheese; bake, uncovered, in moderately hot oven about 10 minutes or until cheese is melted. **Meanwhile,** mash avocado with fork in medium bowl. Add half the sour cream and the juice; mix well.
To serve, put spoonfuls of avocado mixture and remaining sour cream over the nachos.

Serves 4 to 6

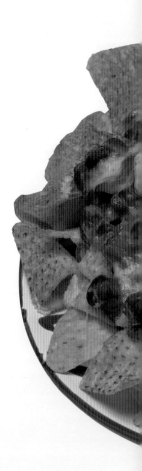

6 nutty chicken
wings

12 chicken wings (1kg)

2 teaspoons vegetable oil

2 cloves garlic, crushed

2 teaspoons mild curry powder

$1/3$ cup (85g) smooth peanut butter

$1/4$ cup (60ml) soy sauce

$1/2$ cup (125ml) plum sauce

1 tablespoon water

Remove and discard wing tips from chicken wings.
Heat oil in small saucepan; cook garlic and curry powder, stirring, until fragrant. Stir in peanut butter, sauces and water; cook, stirring, 3 minutes.
Pour peanut butter mixture over chicken wings in large bowl; mix well. Cover, refrigerate 3 hours or overnight.
Place chicken wings in oiled baking dish; brush with marinade. Bake, uncovered, in moderately hot oven about 35 minutes or until browned all over and cooked through.
Makes 12

seafood

spring rolls

8 seafood sticks, chopped finely

2 tablespoons finely chopped fresh coriander leaves

1 large carrot (180g), grated coarsely

310g can corn kernels, drained

300g can water chestnuts, drained, chopped

1 teaspoon sesame oil

8 x 25cm square spring roll wrappers

50g butter, melted

Combine seafood sticks, coriander, carrot, corn, chestnuts and sesame oil in medium bowl. Spoon one-eighth of the mixture across corner of each wrapper; brush edges with a little of the butter. Tuck in ends and roll up to enclose filling.

Place spring rolls on oiled oven tray; brush with remaining butter. Bake, uncovered, in very hot oven about 10 minutes or until browned lightly and heated through. Serve with soy sauce, if desired.

Makes 8

8 honeyed
drumsticks

12 chicken drumsticks
(1.8kg)

2 cloves garlic,
crushed

1 teaspoon grated
fresh ginger

$^1/_3$ cup (80ml) soy
sauce

$^1/_3$ cup (80ml) honey

2 tablespoons water

1 teaspoon sesame oil

Combine chicken with remaining ingredients in
large shallow ovenproof dish; mix well to coat
chicken with honey mixture. Bake, uncovered,
in moderate oven about 40 minutes or until
chicken is browned and cooked through, turning
once during cooking.

Makes 12

traffic light 9

sandwiches

12 slices wholemeal bread

2 tablespoons cheese spread

6 cherry tomatoes

2 slices processed cheddar cheese

2 gherkins, sliced

Cut crusts from bread; discard crusts. Cut bread in half to form 24 rectangles. Spread cheese spread over 12 of the rectangles; set aside.

Using a 2cm round cutter, cut out three rounds, in a straight line, from each of the remaining rectangles to form front of traffic lights. Cut thin slices from each end of the cherry tomatoes; keep centres for another use.

Place a tomato end, a 2cm square of cheese, then a slice of gherkin on a cheese spread-covered rectangle. Top with a traffic light front; adjust tomato, cheese and gherkin to line up with holes. Repeat with remaining bread and fillings.

Makes 12

10 chicken and corn

turnovers

1 tablespoon vegetable oil

500g minced chicken

1 medium red capsicum (200g), chopped finely

310g can creamed corn

2 green onions, chopped finely

6 sheets ready-rolled puff pastry

1 egg, beaten lightly

Heat oil in medium saucepan; cook chicken, stirring, until browned. Add capsicum; cook, stirring, until tender. Remove from heat; stir in corn and onion, cool.

Cut four 11cm rounds from each pastry sheet. Divide chicken mixture among rounds; spread carefully, leaving a 1cm border. Brush pastry edges with egg; fold over to enclose filling. Press edges together to seal.

Place turnovers on oiled oven trays; brush with egg. Bake, uncovered, in hot oven about 15 minutes or until browned lightly.

Makes 24

super banana peanut butter roll-ups

¹/₃ cup (85g) smooth peanut butter

2 tablespoons honey or Nutella

2 large pitta, halved

2 medium bananas (400g), sliced

Spread peanut butter and honey on one side of pitta. Top with banana; roll up.

Makes 4

golden

fish bites

250g boneless white fish fillets, chopped roughly

2 green onions, chopped finely

2 teaspoons soy sauce

1 egg white

1 teaspoon cornflour

15 slices day-old white bread

vegetable oil, for deep-frying

sauce

2 teaspoons cornflour

2 tablespoons lemon juice

1 teaspoon soy sauce

$1/2$ cup (125ml) chicken stock

1 green onion, chopped finely

Blend or process fish until finely minced. Transfer fish to medium bowl; add onion, sauce, egg white and cornflour, mix well.

Remove crusts from bread; flatten as much as possible by rolling with glass bottle or rolling pin. Freeze; using sharp knife, cut frozen bread into 5mm cubes. Using damp hands, roll level teaspoons of fish mixture into balls; toss in bread cubes. Press cubes on firmly; cover. Refrigerate 30 minutes.

Just before serving, deep-fry fish bites in hot oil until browned lightly and cooked through; drain on absorbent paper. Serve with Sauce.

Sauce Blend cornflour with juice in small saucepan; add remaining ingredients. Stir over heat until sauce boils and thickens slightly.

Makes about 40

just **cheese**

pizza

27cm packaged pizza base

1/4 cup (60ml) tomato paste

1/2 cup (50g) coarsely grated mozzarella cheese

1/2 cup (60g) coarsely grated cheddar cheese

1/2 cup (40g) finely grated parmesan cheese

Place pizza base on pizza tray or large oven tray; spread with tomato paste. Top with combined cheeses. Bake, uncovered, in hot oven about 8 minutes or until cheese is melted and browned lightly.

Serves 2 to 4

chip-crumbed chicken

drumsticks

6 chicken drumsticks (900g)

plain flour

2 eggs, beaten lightly

1/3 cup (35g) packaged breadcrumbs

150g packet plain potato crisps, crushed

1/3 cup (25g) finely grated parmesan cheese

1 teaspoon chicken stock powder

2 tablespoons chopped fresh parsley

Coat chicken drumsticks in flour, shake off excess. Dip in egg, then combined breadcrumbs, crisps, cheese, stock powder and parsley, pressing crumb mixture on firmly. Place chicken on oiled oven tray. Cover, refrigerate 30 minutes.

Bake, uncovered, in moderate oven about 50 minutes or until chicken is browned all over and cooked through.

Serve hot or cold.

Makes 6

16 cheese and bacon
potatoes

15 tiny new potatoes (600g)

120g camembert cheese, chopped finely

2 tablespoons finely grated parmesan cheese

2 bacon rashers, chopped finely

1 tablespoon finely chopped fresh sage leaves

2 tablespoons packaged breadcrumbs

1/4 cup (20g) finely grated parmesan cheese, extra

Makes 30

Boil, steam or microwave potatoes until just tender; drain, cool. Meanwhile, cook bacon in small frying pan, stirring, until crisp; drain, cool. Cut potatoes in half. Using a melon baller, scoop out most of the potato flesh. Mash flesh; reserve.
Trim bases of potatoes so they sit flat; place on oiled oven tray. Combine reserved potato with camembert, parmesan, bacon, sage and breadcrumbs in small bowl. Spoon mixture into potato halves; sprinkle with extra parmesan. Bake in moderately hot oven about 15 minutes or until heated through.

marinated

chicken wings

12 chicken wings (1kg)

$1/2$ cup (125ml)
barbecue sauce

$1/4$ cup (60ml) soy
sauce

1 tablespoon peanut
oil

$1/2$ teaspoon ground
ginger

Remove and discard wing tips from chicken wings. Combine chicken wings with remaining ingredients in large bowl; mix well. Cover, refrigerate 3 hours or overnight.

Drain chicken over medium bowl; reserve marinade. Place chicken wings in oiled baking dish; bake, uncovered, in moderate oven about 45 minutes or until chicken is browned and cooked through, brushing occasionally with reserved marinade.

Makes 12

18   potato

puffs

2 medium potatoes
(400g), chopped
coarsely

2 teaspoons olive oil

2 bacon rashers,
chopped finely

1 tablespoon finely
chopped fresh chives

130g can corn kernels,
drained

$1/2$ cup (60g) coarsely
grated cheddar cheese

2 eggs, separated

$1/2$ teaspoon sweet
paprika

Lightly oil a 12-hole deep patty pan.
Boil, steam or microwave potato until tender;
drain. Mash; cool slightly.
Heat oil in small saucepan; cook bacon, stirring,
until crisp. Drain on absorbent paper.
Combine potato, bacon, chives, corn, cheese
and egg yolks in medium bowl; mix well.
Beat egg whites in small bowl with electric mixer
or rotary beater until soft peaks form; gently fold
into potato mixture.
Spoon potato mixture into prepared pan;
sprinkle with paprika. Bake, uncovered, in
moderately hot oven about 20 minutes or until
browned lightly and cooked through.

Makes 12

sausage
rolls

500g sausage mince

1 medium brown
onion (150g), grated
coarsely

1 teaspoon mixed
dried herbs

$^3/_4$ cup (75g)
packaged
breadcrumbs

1 egg,
beaten
lightly

2 sheets
ready-rolled
puff pastry

Combine sausage mince with onion, herbs, breadcrumbs and egg in medium bowl; mix well.

Cut pastry sheets in half.

Divide mince mixture into four portions; shape each portion into a sausage shape, the same length as long side of pastry rectangles. Place one mince log on each pastry rectangle. Brush edges of pastry with water; roll pastry over mince logs. Press edges together to seal.

Cut each pastry roll into three pieces; cut two small slits in top of each sausage roll. Place on oiled oven tray; brush lightly with water. Bake, uncovered, in moderately hot oven about 25 minutes or until cooked through.

Makes 12

20 critter

burgers

Ask your butcher to cut ribs into 10cm lengths, then into single rib pieces. You will need 36 single rib pieces for this recipe.

36 American-style pork spare ribs (about 1.5kg)

500g minced pork

2 cups (140g) stale breadcrumbs

4 green onions, chopped finely

2 teaspoons grated fresh ginger

1 tablespoon soy sauce

6 pimiento-stuffed green olives, halved

1/2 medium tomato (190g), seeded, sliced

alfalfa sprouts

parsley sprigs

marinade

2 tablespoons lemon juice

2 cloves garlic, crushed

3/4 cup (180ml) barbecue sauce

1 medium brown onion (150g), grated coarsely

2 tablespoons soy sauce

Combine rib pieces and Marinade in large bowl. Cover, refrigerate 3 hours or overnight.
Combine mince, breadcrumbs, onion, ginger and sauce in large bowl. Shape mixture into six burgers.
Drain ribs over medium bowl; reserve Marinade. Cook burgers and ribs in batches on an oiled grill plate (or grill or barbecue) until both are browned all over and cooked through, brushing with reserved Marinade occasionally during cooking.
Arrange burgers and ribs on plates, as pictured; decorate with remaining ingredients.
Marinade Combine ingredients in large bowl.

Makes 6

22 hot dogs

with special sauce

6 frankfurts

1 tablespoon vegetable oil

3 medium brown onions (450g), sliced thinly

6 hot dog rolls

1¹/₂ cups (185g) coarsely grated cheddar cheese

special sauce

¹/₂ cup (125ml) tomato sauce

2 teaspoons Worcestershire sauce

1 tablespoon brown sugar

1 teaspoon seeded mustard

1 teaspoon malt vinegar

1 clove garlic, crushed

Place frankfurts in large saucepan; cover with cold water. Bring to boil, uncovered; drain.

Heat oil in large frying pan; cook onion, stirring, about 10 minutes or until very soft.

Split rolls in half; place frankfurts in rolls. Top with Special Sauce, onion and cheese.

Special Sauce Combine ingredients in small bowl.

Makes 6

5 school-size pitta breads

1/3 cup (80ml) tomato paste

150g cabanossi, sliced

100g sliced leg ham, sliced

440g can pineapple pieces in natural juice, drained

2 cups (250g) coarsely grated cheddar cheese

Spread pitta breads with tomato paste; top with cabanossi, ham, pineapple and cheese. Bake, uncovered, in hot oven about 10 minutes or until cheese is melted.

Makes 5

24 wedges
with creamy avocado dip

4 medium potatoes (800g), unpeeled

1 tablespoon olive oil

1 tablespoon chicken seasoning

cooking oil spray

creamy avocado dip

2 medium avocados (500g)

$1/4$ cup (60ml) bottled Caesar salad dressing

1 tablespoon lemon juice

Wash and scrub potatoes; pat dry with absorbent paper. Cut potatoes in half; cut each half into four wedges. Combine wedges, oil and seasoning in medium bowl. Coat large baking dish with cooking oil spray; place wedges in dish. Bake, uncovered, in hot oven about 40 minutes or until browned lightly and tender. Serve wedges with Creamy Avocado Dip.
Creamy Avocado Dip Blend or process ingredients until smooth.

Makes 32

crunchy chicken nuggets

5 chicken thigh fillets (550g)

plain flour

1 egg, beaten lightly

1 tablespoon milk

1/4 cup (20g) finely grated parmesan cheese

2/3 cup (70g) Corn Flake Crumbs

1 tablespoon chicken stock powder

Cut chicken into 3cm pieces. Coat chicken pieces in flour, shake off excess. Dip in combined egg and milk, then combined cheese, crumbs and stock powder, pressing crumb mixture on firmly.

Place chicken nuggets, in single layer, on wire rack over oven tray. Bake, uncovered, in moderately hot oven about 30 minutes or until browned lightly and cooked through. Serve nuggets with tomato or barbecue sauce, if desired.

Makes about 20

26 cheesy
mini burgers

6 slices bread

60g butter, melted

1 tablespoon tomato paste

$1/3$ cup (40g) coarsely grated
cheddar cheese

patties

250g minced beef

1 small brown onion (80g),
chopped finely

$1/2$ teaspoon French mustard

$1/2$ teaspoon tomato sauce

$1/2$ teaspoon Worcestershire sauce

Cut four 4.5cm rounds from each slice
of bread. Brush rounds with butter;
place on oven tray. Bake, uncovered,
in moderate oven about 15 minutes
or until crisp. Spread rounds with
tomato paste, top with patties; sprinkle
with cheese. Just before serving, grill
burgers until cheese is melted.
Patties Combine ingredients in
medium bowl. Shape two rounded
teaspoons of mixture into 4cm patties.
Cook patties, in batches, in heated
oiled non-stick pan, until browned
both sides and cooked through.

Makes 24

party games

These party games for young children are a great way to teach kids about winning, losing, fairness and luck. Keep children enthusiastic by moving on to a new game if they begin to appear irritable.

hunt the thimble

Use a small object such as a thimble or ring for this game. It is given to one child and all the other children leave the room. The child with the thimble hides it in the room (or on himself) and then calls the other children back into the room to hunt for the thimble. The person who finds the thimble wins a prize, then it's his turn to hide the thimble.

pin the tail on the donkey

The party girl or boy draws a large picture of a donkey (or a pig or dog or any favourite animal) on a sheet of butcher's paper or cardboard. The animal should have no tail.

A tail is made from a piece of cardboard, strands of wool or a piece of cloth and a drawing pin is inserted in one end. The donkey picture is tacked onto the wall. A party guest is blindfolded, turned around a few times and placed in front of the donkey. He is given the tail and attempts to pin it in the correct position. The party organiser marks the position with the guest's initials. Then it's the next guest's turn. The player who pins the tail nearest the rear end of the donkey wins the game.

the doughnut game

A length of clothes line or string is tied up above the children's heads and doughnuts are hung down from it on pieces of string. Each child must stand under a doughnut and with her hands behind her back try to catch the swinging doughnut in her mouth.

30 rocky road

1 cup (150g) unsalted roasted peanuts, toasted

1/3 cup (25g) shredded coconut, toasted

3 1/3 cups (500g) milk chocolate Melts, melted

4 cups (240g) small multicoloured marshmallows

Grease 20cm x 30cm lamington pan; line base and two long sides with baking paper, extending paper 2cm above edge of pan.

Combine ingredients in large bowl; spread into prepared pan. Cover, refrigerate until set. Cut or break into five squares.

honey joys

100g butter

¹/₄ cup (55g) caster sugar

1 tablespoon honey

4 cups (120g) Corn Flakes

Line two 12-hole deep patty pans with paper patty cases.

Combine butter, sugar and honey in small saucepan; stir over heat, without boiling, until sugar is dissolved. Bring to boil; remove from heat.

Place Corn Flakes in large bowl, add honey mixture; stir gently to combine. Spoon mixture into paper cases. Bake in moderate oven 10 minutes; cool.

Makes 24

choc-chip butterfly
cakes

60g butter

1 teaspoon vanilla essence

$1/3$ cup (75g) caster sugar

$3/4$ cup (110g) self-raising flour

$1/4$ cup (60ml) milk

1 egg

$1/4$ cup (45g) dark Choc Bits

$2/3$ cup (160ml) thickened cream

1 tablespoon icing sugar mixture

2 red glacé cherries, sliced

icing sugar mixture, extra

Line a 12-hole deep patty pan with paper patty cases.

Beat butter, essence, sugar, flour, milk and egg in small bowl with electric mixer on low speed until combined.

Bevat on medium speed until mixture is smooth and changed to a lighter colour.

Stir in Choc Bits.

Spoon mixture into prepared cases. Bake in moderate oven about 20 minutes. Turn onto wire rack to cool. Cut shallow 4cm rounds from tops of cakes.

Beat cream and icing sugar in small bowl with electric mixer or rotary beater until soft peaks form.

Spoon cream mixture into holes in cakes; top with halved cake tops and cherry pieces. Sift extra icing sugar over cakes.

Makes 12

34 popcorn
caramels

¹/₄ cup (60ml) vegetable oil

¹/₃ cup (80g) popping corn

150g butter, chopped

250g packet Jersey caramels

Line 12-hole (¹/₃ cup/80ml) muffin pan with paper-lined foil muffin cases.

Heat oil in large saucepan; add corn. Cover with tight-fitting lid; shake pan a few times and cook until you can hear only a few popping noises.

Remove from heat; you will need 4 cups popped corn for this recipe. Place popcorn in large bowl.

Place butter and caramels in same pan; cook, stirring, until mixture is smooth. Remove from heat; gently stir in popcorn. Spoon popcorn mixture into cases; cool.

Makes 12

with honey yogurt

200g tub vanilla yogurt

small pinch ground cinnamon

1 tablespoon honey

1 medium banana (200g), sliced thickly

1 tablespoon lemon juice

2 medium kiwi fruit (170g), sliced thickly

250g strawberries, halved

Combine yogurt, cinnamon and honey in medium bowl. **Drizzle** banana with juice. Serve fruit with yogurt mixture.

Serves 4

36 chocolate
macaroon slice

125g butter

200g milk chocolate, chopped

1 cup (70g) shredded coconut

90g packet coconut macaroons, crushed finely

2/3 cup (140g) glacé cherries, chopped finely

2/3 cup (100g) white chocolate Melts, melted

Grease 20cm x 30cm lamington pan; line base and two long sides with baking paper, extending paper 2cm above edge of pan.
Melt butter and milk chocolate in medium heatproof bowl over pan of simmering water. Stir in coconut and macaroon crumbs. Press mixture firmly over base of prepared pan; top with cherries. Drizzle with white chocolate, cover. Refrigerate until firm; cut into squares.

rainbow slice

2¹/₂ cups (250g) plain
chocolate biscuit crumbs

125g butter, melted

400g (300ml) can
sweetened condensed
milk

¹/₂ cup (45g) desiccated
coconut

1 cup (150g) unsalted
roasted peanuts,
chopped

250g packet Smarties

Grease 20cm x 30cm lamington pan. Line
base and two long sides with baking paper,
extending paper 2cm above edge of pan.
Combine biscuit crumbs and butter in
medium bowl; press over base of prepared
pan. Cover, refrigerate 20 minutes.
Combine remaining ingredients in medium
bowl; spread over base. Bake in moderate
oven about 30 minutes or until browned
lightly; cool in pan. Refrigerate slice
before cutting.

party patty

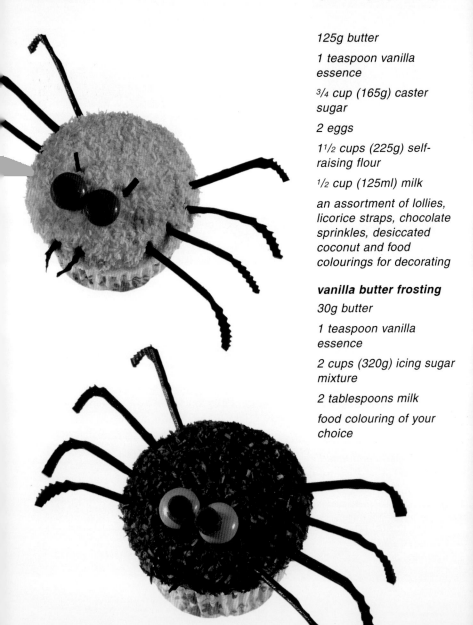

125g butter

1 teaspoon vanilla essence

³/₄ cup (165g) caster sugar

2 eggs

1¹/₂ cups (225g) self-raising flour

¹/₂ cup (125ml) milk

an assortment of lollies, licorice straps, chocolate sprinkles, desiccated coconut and food colourings for decorating

vanilla butter frosting

30g butter

1 teaspoon vanilla essence

2 cups (320g) icing sugar mixture

2 tablespoons milk

food colouring of your choice

Grease two 12-hole deep patty pans; line with paper patty cases. **Beat** butter, essence and sugar in small bowl with electric mixer until light and fluffy. Add eggs, one at a time, beating well after each addition. Transfer mixture to large bowl; stir in flour and milk. Spoon mixture into patty cases.

Bake in moderate oven 15 minutes. Turn onto wire rack to cool. Spread cold cakes with Vanilla Butter Frosting, then decorate with the lollies, licorice straps, chocolate sprinkles and coloured coconut, using our designs as your guide.

Vanilla Butter Frosting Combine butter, essence, half the icing sugar, and half the milk in medium bowl with wooden spoon until smooth. Add remaining icing sugar and milk; beat until smooth. Divide the icing among small bowls and colour each with a few drops of the food colouring of your choice.

To make coloured coconut, put some coconut into a small plastic bag then add a few drops of the food colouring of your choice. Seal the bag then shake it and rub the bag in your hands until the coconut is coloured.

Makes 24

toffees

3 cups (660g) sugar

1 cup (250ml) water

¹/₄ cup (60ml) malt vinegar

coloured sprinkles, if desired

Line (¹/₃ cup/80ml) muffin pans with paper muffin cases.

Combine sugar, the water and vinegar in medium pan, stir over low heat until sugar is dissolved. Bring to boil; boil rapidly, uncovered,without stirring, about 15 minutes or until syrup reaches "crack" stage (154°C on candy thermometer.) (Or, test by dropping a teaspoon of the syrup into a cup of cold water; if it sets and can be cracked almost immediately, it is ready). Remove pan from heat; allow bubbles to subside. Carefully pour syrup into prepared pans. Stand toffees 2 minutes before decorating with sprinkles. Leave to set at room temperaure.

Makes about 15

easy three-ingredient
slice

125g butter

3 cups (390g) toasted muesli

1/2 cup (125ml) golden syrup

Grease 20cm x 30cm lamington pan; line base and two long sides with baking paper, extending paper 2cm above edge of pan.

Melt butter in large saucepan; add muesli and golden syrup; stir over medium heat about 5 minutes or until mixture thickens and is dark golden brown.

Carefully spread into prepared pan; cover, refrigerate until firm before cutting.

toffee apples

Organic apples are best used for this recipe. You will also need 10 thick wooden skewers available from some butchers or cake decorating suppliers.

10 small apples (1.3kg)

4 cups (900g) sugar

1 cup (250ml) water

¹/₃ cup (80ml) glucose syrup

1 teaspoon liquid red food colouring

Rinse apples under cold water. Stand on rack until completely dry; do not rub with a cloth, because it's important to keep the "bloom". Push a skewer three-quarters of the way into each apple at stem end.

Combine sugar, water, glucose and colouring in medium heavy-based pan. Stir over heat, without boiling, until sugar is dissolved. Boil, uncovered, without stirring, about 20 minutes or until mixture reaches "crack" stage (154°C on sugar thermometer). (Or, test by dropping a teaspoon of the syrup into a cup of cold water; if it sets and can be cracked almost immediately, it is ready.)

Remove syrup from heat; stand pan in baking dish of hot water about 1 minute or until bubbles subside. Remove pan from water; tilt pan. Dip and rotate an apple slowly in syrup until apple is completely coated. Twirl apple around a few times before placing onto greased oven tray to set. Repeat with remaining apples and syrup.

Makes 10

44 chocolate bubble
squares

125g butter, melted

1¹/₂ cups (300g) firmly packed brown sugar

2 eggs, beaten lightly

1 cup (35g) Rice Bubbles

³/₄ cup (60g) desiccated coconut

1 cup (150g) self-raising flour

¹/₄ cup (25g) cocoa powder

bubble topping

200g milk chocolate Melts, melted

125g butter, melted

1 cup (35g) Rice Bubbles

Grease 26cm x 32cm Swiss roll pan; line base and two long sides with baking paper, extending paper 2cm above edge of pan.

Combine butter, sugar and eggs in medium bowl; stir in Rice Bubbles, coconut and sifted dry ingredients; spread into prepared pan. Bake in moderate oven about 25 minutes or until firm; cool in pan. Spread with Bubble Topping. Cover, refrigerate until set before cutting into squares.

Bubble Topping Combine ingredients in medium bowl.

giant

peanut cookies

60g butter, chopped

$1/2$ cup (130g) smooth peanut butter

$1/2$ cup (110g) caster sugar

$1/2$ cup (100g) firmly packed brown sugar

1 egg, beaten lightly

250g packet peanut M&Ms

1 cup (150g) self-raising flour

Beat butters and sugars in small bowl with electric mixer until light and fluffy. Add egg; beat until just combined. Stir in M&Ms and flour. Roll $1/4$ cups of mixture into balls; place about 5cm apart on baking paper-covered oven trays. Flatten mixture slightly, pushing M&Ms back into mixture.

Bake in moderate oven about 15 minutes or until browned lightly; cool on trays.

Makes 10

46 frozen carob
bananas

$^1/_2$ cup (35g) shredded coconut, toasted

$^3/_4$ cup (95g) toasted muesli

3 medium bananas (600g)

6 paddle pop sticks

125g milk carob, melted

2 teaspoons vegetable oil

Combine coconut and muesli on oven tray. Cut bananas in half crossways; insert sticks through centre of each banana half. Combine carob and oil in small bowl; brush over bananas, then roll bananas in muesli mixture.
Place bananas on clean tray, cover with foil; freeze until firm.

Makes 6

chewy choc-chunk cookies

2 eggs

1¹/₃ cups (275g) firmly packed brown sugar

¹/₂ cup (125ml) vegetable oil

1 teaspoon vanilla essence

1 cup (150g) plain flour

³/₄ cup (110g) self-raising flour

¹/₂ teaspoon bicarbonate of soda

1 cup (125g) chopped pecans

³/₄ cup (120g) chopped raisins

1 cup (150g) dark chocolate Melts, halved

¹/₂ cup (95g) white Choc Bits

Beat eggs and sugar in small bowl with electric mixer about 1 minute or until changed to a lighter colour. Stir in oil, essence, sifted dry ingredients and remaining ingredients. Cover; refrigerate 1 hour.

Roll rounded tablespoons of mixture into balls; place on greased oven trays, allowing four per tray. Press balls into 6cm rounds.

Bake in moderately hot oven about 10 minutes or until browned lightly. Stand 5 minutes before lifting onto wire racks to cool.

Makes about 20

48 ladybirds

60g butter

1 teaspoon vanilla essence

¹/₄ cup (55g) caster sugar

1 egg

1 tablespoon milk

²/₃ cup (100g) self-raising flour

1 licorice strap

¹/₂ cup (95g) dark Choc Bits, approximately

raspberry icing

3 cups (475g) icing sugar mixture

15g butter

¹/₃ cup (80ml) raspberry-flavoured cordial

Lightly grease 12-hole gem scone iron.

Beat butter, essence, sugar and egg in small bowl with electric mixer until light and fluffy. Stir in milk and flour in two batches.

Spoon mixture into prepared pan. Bake in moderate oven 15 minutes. Turn cakes onto wire rack to cool.

Place six cakes, flat side down, on a wire rack over tray. Spoon half the Raspberry Icing over cakes; decorate with sliced licorice and Choc Bits. Allow to set.

Repeat with remaining six cakes, Raspberry Icing, licorice and Choc Bits.

Raspberry Icing Place icing sugar into a medium heatproof bowl; stir in remaining ingredients. Stir over hot water until a coating consistency.

Makes 12

50 chocolate

mousse

200g dark chocolate, chopped

300ml thickened cream

3 eggs, beaten lightly

1/3 cup (75g) caster sugar

Place chocolate in medium heatproof bowl over pan of simmering water; stir until melted. Remove from heat; cool 10 minutes. Beat cream in small bowl with electric mixer or rotary beater until soft peaks form. Using a whisk, gently fold cream into melted chocolate.

Beat eggs and sugar in small separate bowl with electric mixer until thick and pale; gently fold into chocolate mixture in two batches. Spoon into eight 3/4-cup (180m) serving dishes. Cover; refrigerate until cold and just firm. Serve topped with extra whipped cream, chocolate curls and chocolate-drizzled sponge finger biscuits, if desired.

Makes 8

choc-topped
crunchy slice

3 x 65g Mars Bars, chopped

90g butter

3 cups (105g) Rice Bubbles

topping

200g milk chocolate, chopped

30g butter

Grease 20cm x 30cm lamington pan; line base and two long sides with baking paper, extending paper 2cm above edge of pan.

Combine Mars Bars and butter in large saucepan. Stir over low heat, without boiling, until mixture is smooth; stir in Rice Bubbles. Press mixture into prepared pan; spread with Topping. Refrigerate until set before cutting.

Topping Melt chocolate and butter in small heatproof bowl over pan of simmering water until smooth.

chewy chocolate
coconut slice

125g butter, melted

1 cup (200g) firmly packed brown sugar

1 egg, beaten lightly

1 teaspoon vanilla essence

$1/2$ cup (75g) plain flour

$1/4$ cup (35g) self-raising flour

2 tablespoons cocoa powder

$1/2$ cup (45g) desiccated coconut

1 tablespoon desiccated coconut, extra

chocolate icing

1 cup (160g) icing sugar mixture

2 tablespoons cocoa powder

10g butter, melted

$1^1/2$ tablespoons hot water, approximately

Grease 19cm x 29cm slice pan; line base and two long sides with baking paper, extending paper 2cm above edge of pan.

Combine butter, sugar, egg and essence in medium bowl. Stir in sifted flours, cocoa and coconut; spread over base of prepared pan. Bake in moderate oven about 30 minutes or until firm. Spread hot slice with Chocolate Icing. Sprinkle with extra coconut; cool before cutting into slices.

Chocolate Icing Sift icing sugar and cocoa into medium bowl; add butter and the water. Stir until icing is spreadable.

crunchy choc-topped
breadsticks

1/2 cup (125ml) thickened cream

1 teaspoon icing sugar mixture

1/2 cup (125ml) Nutella

1/2 x 300g packet thin grissini, halved

1/2 cup (75g) chopped mixed nuts

1/2 cup (120g) hundreds and thousands

Beat cream and icing sugar in small bowl with electric mixer or rotary beater until soft peaks form. Stir in Nutella.
Dip the grissini into Nutella mixture, then roll them in the nuts or the hundreds and thousands.

brilliant
brownies

180g butter, melted

³/₄ cup (165g) caster sugar

*³/₄ cup (150g) firmly packed
brown sugar*

3 eggs

¹/₂ cup (75g) plain flour

¹/₃ cup (50g) self-raising flour

¹/₃ cup (35g) cocoa powder

2 teaspoons drinking chocolate

2 teaspoons icing sugar mixture

Grease 19cm x 29cm slice pan;
line base and two long sides
with baking paper, extending paper
2cm above edge of pan.
Whisk butter and sugars in large bowl
until combined. Whisk in eggs, one at
a time, whisking well after each addition.
Whisk in sifted flours and cocoa; pour
mixture into prepared pan.
Bake in moderate oven 15 minutes.
Cover with foil, bake 45 minutes.
Cool in pan; cut into 7cm x 9cm rectangles.
Sift drinking chocolate over half the
brownies and sift the icing sugar over the
remaining brownies.
(We used a plastic stencil to make
the numbers.)

Makes 24

56 fruity
kebabs

4 medium kiwi fruit (340g)

250g strawberries

1 cup (150g) dark chocolate Melts, melted

2 medium bananas (400g), sliced thickly

1 tablespoon lemon juice

$1/2$ cup (45g) desiccated coconut

Cut each kiwi fruit into wedges. Dip half of each strawberry in chocolate; allow to partially set. Dip bananas in juice, then coat in coconut, pressing coconut on firmly.

Thread kiwi fruit, strawberries and banana slices onto eight skewers.

Makes 8

treats

200g butter

400g can sweetened condensed milk

1 cup (200g) firmly packed brown sugar

$^1/_4$ cup (25g) cocoa powder

2 teaspoons vanilla essence

3$^3/_4$ cups (375g) plain sweet biscuit crumbs

3 x 100g packets marshmallows

1$^1/_2$ cups (135g) desiccated coconut

Combine butter, milk, sugar, sifted cocoa and essence in medium saucepan; stir over heat, without boiling, until butter melts. Remove from heat; stir in biscuit crumbs.

Roll three heaped teaspoons of mixture around each marshmallow, using damp hands, pressing firmly to enclose marshmallows. Roll in coconut; place on trays, refrigerate until firm.

Makes about 55

58 meringue
critters

It is normal for meringues to crack a little during cooking. You will need at least two large oven trays for this recipe.

4 egg whites

1 cup (220g) caster sugar

red and green food colouring

licorice, hundreds and thousands and assorted lollies to decorate

Beat egg whites in small bowl with electric mixer until soft peaks form. Gradually add sugar, beating until dissolved between additions. Continue beating on high speed about 10 minutes or until firm peaks form.

Divide mixture into two portions. Stir in a few drops of red food colouring to one portion, and a few drops of green food colouring to remaining portion. Pipe all critters, about 5cm apart, onto greased oven trays covered with baking paper. Decorate with licorice, hundreds and thousands and sweets.

For Ladybirds Spoon red mixture into piping bag fitted with 12mm plain tube; pipe eight 4cm rounds, then smaller rounds, about 1.5cm, joining first round.

For Spiders Pipe two rounds, as for the Ladybirds, but make first round slightly smaller.

For Caterpillars Spoon green mixture into clean piping bag fitted with 12mm plain tube. Pipe caterpillars into a spiral about 8cm long.

For Bees Pipe three rounds all joining each other, making each round progressively smaller than the first.

Bake critters in very slow oven about 45 minutes or until critters are dry to touch. Turn oven off, cool critters in oven with door ajar.

Makes about 30

glossary

bacon rashers also known as bacon slices.

barbecue sauce a spicy, tomato-based sauce used to marinate, baste or as an accompaniment.

breadcrumbs

packaged: fine textured, crunchy, purchased white breadcrumbs.

stale: one-or two-day-old bread made into crumbs by grating, blending or processing.

butter use salted or unsalted ("sweet") butter; 125g is equal to 1 stick butter.

cabanossi a ready-to-eat sausage; also known as cabana.

capsicum also known as bell pepper, sweet pepper or, simply, pepper. Seeds and membranes should be discarded before use.

carob imitation chocolate; available in light and dark powder, also in block form. Can be purchased in health food stores.

chicken seasoning a packaged mix of herbs and spices including sweet paprika, garlic, ginger and black pepper.

chilli sauce, sweet a mild Thai-type commercial sauce made from red chillies, sugar, garlic and vinegar.

chips, potato

also known as potato crisps or just chips. May be crushed and used as a crumb coating.

chocolate

bits: also known as chocolate chips and chocolate morsels; available in milk, white and dark chocolate. They hold their shape in baking and are ideal for decorating.

dark: also called bittersweet and plain chocolate. Good quality eating chocolate with low sugar content.

melts: discs of compound chocolate available in milk, white and dark chocolate. They are ideal for melting or moulding.

milk: this contains milk powder or condensed milk and usually has a lower percentage of cocoa than dark chocolate, but more sugar.

white: made from cocoa butter and milk, it contains no chocolate liquor, which is why it's white.

drinking: sweetened cocoa powder.

coconut macaroons small biscuits based on meringue and coconut mixture.

cordial sugar fruit-flavoured syrup that is added to water as a drink.

Corn Flakes breakfast cereal made from toasted corn.

Corn Flake crumbs a packaged product of crushed Corn Flakes used to coat chicken etc.

cornflour also known as cornstarch.

custard powder packaged, vanilla pudding mixture.

dressing, Ranch bottled dressing available in supermarkets.

essence also known as extracts; generally the by-product of distillation of plants.

fish fillets, white white-fleshed, non-oily fish pieces that have been boned and skinned.

food colourings available in liquid, powdered and concentrated paste forms.

frankfurts a smoked, seasoned, precooked sausage made from beef, pork, veal, chicken or turkey.

gelatine we use powdered gelatine. It is also available in sheet form known as leaf gelatine.

gherkins sometimes known as cornichon; young, dark green cucumbers grown especially for pickling.

ginger

fresh: also known as green or root ginger; the thick gnarled root of a tropical plant.

ground: also known as powdered ginger; used as a flavouring in cakes, pies and puddings but cannot be substituted for fresh ginger.

glucose syrup also known as liquid glucose; a sugary syrup obtained from starches such as wheat and corn. Used in confectionery-making to prevent crystallisation.

golden syrup a by-product of refined sugarcane; pure maple syrup or honey can be substituted.

green onion also known as scallions or (incorrectly) shallot; an immature onion picked before the bulb has formed, having a long, green edible stalk.

grissini, mini Italian for "breadstick"; thin, small, crisp breadsticks.

herbs, mixed 1 teaspoon of dried (not ground) is equal to 4 teaspoons chopped fresh herbs.

hundred and thousands tiny, brightly coloured sugary balls, used for decoration.

lamb riblets a cut of meat from a rib end of lamb.

Mexibeans the trade name for a canned mixture of pinto beans and chilli sauce.

mustard, seeded also known as wholegrain. A French-style coarse-grain mustard made from crushed mustard seeds and Dijon-style French mustard.

Nutella a chocolate and hazelnut spread.

oil

cooking spray: vegetable oil in an aerosol can.

olive: mono-unsaturated; made from the pressing of tree-ripened olives. Especially good for everyday cooking and as an ingredient.

peanut: pressed from ground peanuts; most commonly used oil in Asian cooking because of its high smoke point.

sesame: made from roasted, crushed, white sesame seeds; a flavouring rather than a cooking medium.

vegetable: any of a number of oils sourced from plants rather than animal fats.

oven fries (frozen) thin strips of frozen potato.

peanut M&Ms peanuts coated in chocolate with a candy shell.

plum sauce a thick, sweet-and-sour condiment made with plums, sugar, vinegar and apples.

pork, American-style spare ribs well-trimmed mid-loin ribs.

Rice Bubbles breakfast cereal of puffed grains of rice.

sausage mince ground pork or other meat mixed with fat, salt and various seasonings, and sold without the sausage casing; used for meatloaf and terrines.

seafood sticks made from processed Alaskan pollack flavoured with crab.

strawberry jelly crystals fruit flavoured gelatine crystals available from supermarkets.

sugar

We use coarse, granulated table sugar, also known as crystal sugar, unless otherwise specified.

brown: an extremely soft, fine granulated sugar retaining molasses for its characteristic colour and flavour.

caster: also known as superfine or granulated table sugar.

icing sugar mixture: also known as confectioners' sugar or powdered sugar; granulated sugar crushed together with a small amount (about 3%) cornflour added.

sugar crystals, coloured granulated sugar, that has been coloured with food colouring.

taco sauce, mild packaged seasoning meant to duplicate the Mexican sauce made from oregano, cumin, chillies and other spices.

tomato

paste: a concentrated tomato puree used to flavour soups, stews, sauces and casseroles.

sauce: also known as ketchup or catsup; a flavoured condiment made from tomatoes, vinegar and spices.

index

facts and figures 63

These conversions are approximate only, but the difference between an exact and the approximate conversion of various liquid and dry measures is minimal and will not affect your cooking results.

Measuring equipment

The difference between one country's measuring cups and another's is, at most, within a 2 or 3 teaspoon variance. (For the record, 1 Australian metric measuring cup holds approximately 250ml.) The most accurate way of measuring dry ingredients is to weigh them. For liquids, use a clear glass or plastic jug having metric markings.

Note: NZ, Canada, USA and UK all use 15ml tablespoons. Australian tablespoons measure 20ml.
All cup and spoon measurements are level.

How to measure

When using graduated measuring cups, shake dry ingredients loosely into the appropriate cup. Do not tap the cup on a bench or tightly pack the ingredients unless directed to do so. Level the top of measuring cups and measuring spoons with a knife. When measuring liquids, place a clear glass or plastic jug having metric markings on a flat surface to check accuracy at eye level.

Dry Measures

metric	imperial
15g	1/2 oz
30g	1oz
60g	2oz
90g	3oz
125g	4oz (1/4 lb)
155g	5oz
185g	6oz
220g	7oz
250g	8oz (1/2 lb)
280g	9oz
315g	10oz
345g	11oz
375g	12oz (3/4 lb)
410g	13oz
440g	14oz
470g	15oz
500g	16oz (1lb)
750g	24oz (1 1/2 lb)
1kg	32oz (2lb)

We use large eggs having an average weight of 60g.

Liquid Measures

metric	imperial
30ml	1 fluid oz
60ml	2 fluid oz
100ml	3 fluid oz
125ml	4 fluid oz
150ml	5 fluid oz (1/4 pint/1 gill)
190ml	6 fluid oz
250ml (1cup)	8 fluid oz
300ml	10 fluid oz (1/2 pint)
500ml	16 fluid oz
600ml	20 fluid oz (1 pint)
1000ml (1litre)	1 3/4 pints

Helpful Measures

metric	imperial
3mm	1/8 in
6mm	1/4 in
1cm	1/2 in
2cm	3/4 in
2.5cm	1in
6cm	2 1/2 in
8cm	3in
20cm	8in
23cm	9in
25cm	10in
30cm	12in (1ft)

Oven Temperatures

These oven temperatures are only a guide. Always check the manufacturer's manual.

	°C (Celsius)	°F (Fahrenheit)	Gas Mark
Very slow	120	250	1
Slow	150	300	2
Moderately slow	160	325	3
Moderate	180 –190	350 – 375	4
Moderately hot	200 – 210	400 – 425	5
Hot	220 – 230	450 – 475	6
Very hot	240 – 250	500 – 525	7

at your fingertips

These elegant slipcovers store up to 10 mini books and make the books instantly accessible.

And the metric measuring cups and spoons make following our recipes a piece of cake.

Book Holder
Australia and overseas:
$8.95 (incl. GST).

Metric Measuring Set
Australia: $6.50 (incl. GST).
New Zealand: $8.00.
Elsewhere: $9.95.
Prices include postage and handling. This offer is available in all countries.

Mail or fax Photocopy and complete the coupon below and post to
ACP Books Reader Offer,
ACP Publishing, GPO Box 4967,
Sydney NSW 2001, or fax to (02) 9267 4967.

Phone Have your credit card details ready, then phone 136 116 (Mon-Fri, 8.00am-6.00pm; Sat, 8.00am-6.00pm).

Australian residents We accept the credit cards listed on the coupon, money orders and cheques.

Overseas residents We accept the credit cards listed on the coupon, drafts in $A drawn on an Australian bank, and also UK, NZ and US cheques in the currency of the country of issue. Credit card charges are at the exchange rate current at the time of payment.

Photocopy and complete coupon below

Food director Pamela Clark
Food editor Louise Patniotis
Assistant recipe editor Elizabeth Hooper
ACP BOOKS
Editorial director Susan Tomnay
Creative director Hieu Chi Nguyen
Designer Jackie Richards
Studio manager Caryl Wiggins
Publishing manager (sales) Brian Cearnes
Sales & marketing coordinator Caroline Lowry
Publishing manager (rights & new projects) Jane Hazell
Brand manager Sarah Cave
Pre-press by Harry Palmer
Production manager Carol Currie
Business Manager Seymour Cohen
Business analyst Martin Howes
Chief executive officer John Alexander
Group publisher Pat Ingram
Publisher Sue Wannan
Editor-in-chief Deborah Thomas

Produced by ACP Books, Sydney.
Printing by Dai Nippon Printing in Korea.
Published by ACP Publishing Pty Limited, 54 Park St, Sydney;
GPO Box 4088, Sydney, NSW 2001.
Ph: (02) 9282 8618 Fax: (02) 9267 9438.
www.acpbooks.com.au
To order books phone 136 116.
Send recipe enquiries to
Recipeenquiries@acp.com.au
Australia Distributed by Network Services, GPO Box 4088, Sydney, NSW 2001.
Ph: (02) 9282 8777 Fax: (02) 9264 3278.
United Kingdom Distributed by Australian Consolidated Press (UK), Moulton Park Business Centre, Red House Road, Moulton Park, Northampton, NN3 6AQ. Ph: (01604) 497 531
Fax: (01604) 497 533 acpukltd@aol.com
Canada Distributed by Whitecap Books Ltd, 351 Lynn Ave, North Vancouver, BC, V7J 2C4,
Ph: (604) 980 9852 Fax: (604) 980 8197
customerservice@whitecap.ca
www.whitecap.ca
New Zealand Distributed by Netlink Distribution Company, ACP Media Centre, Cnr Fanshawe and Beaumont Streets, Westhaven, Auckland; PO Box 47906, Ponsonby, Auckland, NZ.
Ph: (09) 366 9966 ask@ndcnz.co.nz
South Africa Distributed by PSD Promotions, 30 Diesel Road, Isando, Gauteng, Johannesburg; PO Box 1175, Isando, 1600, Gauteng, Johannesburg. Ph: (27 11) 392 6065/7
Fax: (27 11) 392 6079/80 orders@psdprom.co.za

Kids' Party Food
Includes index.
ISBN 1 86396 180 1.

1. Cookery. 2. Children's parties.
I Title: Australian Women's Weekly.
641.568

© ACP Publishing Pty Limited 2000
ACN 053 273 546
ABN 18 053 273 546

Cover Mini pizza, page 23; Wedges with creamy avocado dip, page 24; Chocolate rainbow slice, page 37; Crunchy choc-topped breadsticks, page 54.

Stylist Sarah O'Brien
Photographer Scott Cameron
Back cover on left, Chicken and corn turnover, page 10; on right, Ladybirds, page 48.

First published 2000. Reprinted 2004.